R U OK?

Kristi Hugstad

First published by Dog Ear Publishing
4011 Vincennes Rd
Indianapolis, IN 46268
www.dogearpublishing.net

ISBN: 978-1-4575-5463-6

This book is printed on acid-free paper.

Printed in the United States of America

Dedication

To struggling teens everywhere. You are not alone.

"The most beautiful people we have known are those who have known defeat, known suffering, known struggle, known loss, and have found their way out of the depths. These persons have an appreciation, a sensitivity, and an understanding of life that fills them with compassion, gentleness, and a deep loving concern. "

-Elisabeth Kübler-Ross

I Might Be Like You or Someone You Know

Hi, my name is Gavin, and that's my face you see on the cover of this book. What that picture doesn't show is how much I've been through in my life.

I suffer from depression and I've been seriously suicidal, yet I'm still here, right now, today, and I'm actually happy. But that wasn't always the case.

So why am I still here? Or more importantly, how?

I'm here because I got treatment for my depression. Once I realized I had this illness and got help for it, life got better.

But I get ahead of myself.

When I was just four years old, my dad died from lung cancer. I remember visiting him in the hospital, having no clue what was going on (how could I? I was only four), and then one day, my dad was just gone. Forever. I can't recall a single childhood birthday party. My mom struggled as a single mother to raise my two brothers and me. I know it wasn't easy for her or for any of us.

By the time I got to middle school, I had severe depression and anxiety, but I didn't know it. I had no desire to go to school and when I got home, all I did was sleep. I went to counseling, but it didn't help my depression. The older I got, the darker my world got. In high school I began to use benzos and other prescription drugs. They gave me some immediate relief, but that didn't last.

If I had to sum it up, I'd say I felt like I was a total waste of space. I felt as if I didn't have a purpose. I was suicidal. I went to the top of a parking structure in Mission Viejo, California. Jumping off seemed like the best way to escape my pain. It wasn't that I wanted so much to end my life as I wanted to stop hurting on the inside so badly.

As I stood there contemplating my death, I looked up and saw a sign for the Mission Hospital. It seemed to call to me, telling me to come inside and get help. I went into detox for five days, followed by treatment for six months, and then I continued therapy for one year.

Do you know what happened?

I began to realize that my life matters.

See, I didn't know what depression looked like, I just thought something was terribly wrong with me. My brain was crying for help and once I got help, life improved a heck of a lot. Had I been taught the warning signs of depression, my high school experience may have been different.

I now have the coping skills to deal with my depression. When I feel down, I know that tomorrow will be a better day. I'm doing what I love, and I'm surrounded by family and friends who love me, too.

Maybe you hurt like I did, or maybe you know someone who sounds like who I used to be. If you do, this book is for you.

This book has all of the information that I wish I'd had during my darkest of times. Depression is a disease that can be treated.

Whether it's you or a friend, there is treatment and hope. Things can turn around.

You've picked up this book, and that's a huge first step. Good for you! Now turn the page, and learn more about how to help yourself or other people who might be – a little or a lot – like I used to be.

Wishing you all the best,

Gavin

Listen Up

Being a teenager in this day and age is totally exhausting.

Your parents and teachers were once teenagers (hard to believe, right?) but they didn't have laptops, smart phones and social media. They didn't have to *keep up*. So they get it, but maybe not entirely, not the way you do because you're *in* it. And you're in deep – you can't avoid it – you can't just *not* be who you are or where you are! There are times you just want to go in your bedroom, shut the door and not have to deal with anyone ever again.

It's only human to reach your breaking point sometimes with people, school, friends, family, *life*. But when that breaking point feels like a tunnel without a light at the end, when it feels like you are very alone and no one cares, when it feels like you are only spiraling further downward, that's cause for concern – that's when a problem might be hard to solve completely on your own. That's when you need help – which is totally okay. Everyone – poor, rich, old, young, black, white – absolutely everyone needs help in life once in a while. No one can go it alone all the way.

Maybe you picked up this book because you're looking for information about help with depression or suicide for yourself, a friend or family member. Or maybe someone at your school asked you to read this book. Whatever the reason, I hope I can help you find the information you are looking for.

You might be wondering who I think I am, talking to you like this. Well, here's why I think I might be able to help you: Bill, my husband, completed suicide.

Yes, you read that right.

It was awful, horrible, painful. In fact, these words will never even begin to accurately describe the experience. I'll share the story with you in a little bit. But the experience has made me want to help people who suffer from depression and may be considering suicide – or know someone who suffers from depression and is suicidal – find the appropriate treatment in order to feel better.

When you understand that depression is a disease of your mind, it loses some of its power over you. Yes, depression is very real and very scary, and suicidal thoughts can make you feel frightened and overwhelmed. You might think you're "going crazy" or feel embarrassed to share with others what you are thinking. Or maybe you've tried to talk about how you feel and no one has taken you seriously. Maybe the people you talked to didn't know what to say, so they just said nothing.

This doesn't mean you should give up. Talking about your depressive or suicidal thoughts and feelings with the *right* person will make all the difference in the world.

When you're in a scary place, you're always better off when you are with someone.

Unfortunately, more than 44,000 Americans die by suicide each year. That's a lot of suffering. The truth is, many of us think about suicide at one time or another in our lives – maybe even you. Usually when this happens it's because we are struggling with problems in our lives that seem overwhelming and make us feel trapped and hopeless. It may not be that we really want to die, but just that we want to stop feeling so miserable.

So if you feel depressed, angry or hopeless, try to understand that these feelings usually stem from fear. And what you, your friends or family members don't need right now is more fear on top of how you're already feeling. You may be scared to admit your feelings in case your parents, teachers or peers think you shouldn't be feeling that way. What you need is to accept your emotions, and it just might help to practice acceptance of everyone in your life as well.

In fact, let's go back to that technology and social media thing again. I mean, it's great that we're all so incredibly connected with the touch or swipe of a finger. Yet these conveniences can actually contribute to our feelings of anxiety and insecurity. It's impossible to have anonymity or control over what our peers say about us on social media, and that's just not right. We tend to depend on our peers' approval and, simultaneously, to be afraid of losing it. This makes us emotionally vulnerable. Social media has been linked to both depression and to behaviors that are either risk factors or symptoms of the disease: insomnia, bullying, inability to concentrate and low self-esteem.

The chapters in this book will help you understand depression and suicidal thoughts. The good news is many of these thoughts are a normal part of being a teen. But, depending on the scale, frequency and combination of behaviors, these thoughts can indicate a far more dangerous problem. This book will show you that serious depression is an illness and it can be treated.

First, I will help you recognize the warning signs of depression and suicide, using real-life examples of young people who have suffered it firsthand. I will also share with you the myths of teen suicide. Other topics covered in this book are eating disorders, substance abuse, self-harm, bullying and Post-traumatic Stress Disorder (PTSD). You'll find practical exercises that will teach you how to identify quickly and confidently whether you or someone you know is in need of help, and if so, what to do and where to go for it.

Finally, I will tell you the story of my husband's suicide and ask you to identify risk factors and warning signs. At the time of Bill's death, I didn't recognize or understand these warnings. Perhaps if I had, his story may have turned out differently.

I want your story or the story of a peer you care about to be a good one, full of positive experiences. When the road gets tough (as it inevitably will), I want the challenges you face to be experiences you learn and grow from that will only make you stronger. But first and foremost, don't beat yourself up for your feelings. Depression is no one's fault. There is help, and there is hope!

Chapters

What is Depression?

Depression is identified as feelings of intense sadness lasting two weeks or longer. It's not just about feeling sad when things are going wrong; it's about feeling sad when everything is going *right*, too.

Depression can be powerful, and not in the good way.

Depression affects a person's thoughts in such a way that they don't see when or how a problem can be overcome. It leads people to focus mostly on failures and disappointments and to emphasize only the negative side of their situation. Someone with severe depression is unable to see the possibility of a good outcome and may believe he or she will never be happy again, or that things will never be right for them again.

Looking on the "bright side" is often an impossibility for someone suffering from depression. That's because depression is like wearing sunglasses in an already dark room: it completely distorts your thinking. That's why depressed people can't recognize that suicide is a permanent conclusion to a temporary problem. Someone with depression may feel like there's no other way out, no other escape from emotional pain, and no other way to communicate desperate unhappiness. You can't wait and hope that your mood might improve. When you've been feeling down for a long time, it's hard to step back and view your situation objectively.

Sometimes people who feel suicidal may not even realize they are depressed. When it is the depression, and not the situation, that causes someone to see things in a negative way, suicidal thinking is a real concern.

It's important to remember that there's no "cookie cutter" form of depression. Just as each person's situation and struggles vary, so do the ways in which the disease manifests itself. In the following story, you'll see how depression affected a teenager in Baton Rouge, Louisiana. While the details might not sound familiar, her feelings of guilt and hopelessness might.

Jackie's Story

From a young age, Jackie knew she was different than other girls. Not only was she taller and stronger, she also felt comfortable playing sports with boys, shunned skirts and dresses and kept her hair short. She still recalls holding back during recess or other athletic events, fearing she'd be teased for "acting like a boy."

Jackie's father was an alcoholic, and even though she felt worlds different than her mother, her mom was still her best friend. A former dancer and beauty queen, Jackie's mom obsessed over fad diets, exercise videos and food portions. That's why, when Jackie needed help and validation about her body image, she was too ashamed to share her feelings with her.

Jackie suffered from gender confusion, and this was a source of acute anxiety, which soon morphed into depression. She felt that her body and her gender didn't match. Unfortunately, the only way she knew how to deal with her stress was to take control of the one thing she thought mattered to her parents – how she looked. In an effort to be the "perfect female," Jackie would vomit after she ate, going through unhealthy periods of binging following by violent purging.

Bulimia didn't help Jackie's self-esteem. She continued wrestling with extreme feelings of guilt over who she was, what she ate, how she looked and how the rest of the world perceived her. She thought that if she told her parents how she really felt about herself and her body, they would be disappointed or even angry.

Instead of seeking help from those who loved her, Jackie turned to food and substances as coping mechanisms. At times of extreme depression, she'd binge on foods she knew were off-limits: donuts, French fries and milkshakes. Then she'd vomit as much as she could and vow to start over again. To help curb her appetite, she began using a prescription stimulant which she was able to buy from kids at school.

Throughout high school, Jackie continued to slip into a deep clinical depression. She lived day to day with the idea that she couldn't live up to what everyone else expected of her – and that how she truly felt inside was somehow wrong.

When Jackie graduated, she started to take back the reins of her own life. She moved away from her hometown to attend college. In the anonymity of a new place, she felt she could become who she really was. She sought out support groups for gender dysphoria and eating disorders. She met other students she could relate to. She slowly began the process of accepting herself for who she really was. She started eating healthier and better than ever before, finally accepting her size and shape as they were – *hers*.

Today, Jackie is the CFO of a thriving business in Minneapolis. Her struggles growing up propelled her to become an activist in the LBTQ community. She also volunteers with organizations dedicated to helping teens and young adults with eating disorders.

Jackie's advice to others is simple: Never be ashamed of who you are. Accept yourself as you are, right now. Don't tolerate judgment from others just as you would not judge in return. Practice self-care. Strive to be the best person you can be by being more compassionate and helpful to others. Get outside yourself. The smallest act of kindness will do wonders for your self-pride.

Eating Disorders

Like Jackie, many teens today suffer from eating disorders, also called disordered eating. Eating disorders can range from anorexia (avoidance of food) to bulimia (inducing vomiting after eating) to binge eating and compulsive overeating. Although eating disorders are more common in young females, males are also at risk, particularly those who are athletes. Even teens who do not suffer from an eating disorder might occasionally have a preoccupation with food, weight loss, restrictive eating behavior or food phobias.

Risk factors for eating disorders include but are not limited to:

- Close relatives or a family history of eating disorders

- Family members who exhibit a preoccupation with diet and weight loss

- Family history of mental illness

- A perfectionist personality

- A history of anxiety

- Experience with weight-based bullying or discrimination

- LGBTQ youth

- Small or unsupportive social network

Signs or symptoms of eating disorders include but are not limited to:

- Distorted body image (seeing yourself differently than others see you)

- Frequent or constant feelings of hunger

- Avoidance of events or situations that include food

- Social isolation or withdrawal

- Thinning hair, dry skin and broken nails

- Unexplained skipped menstrual periods

- Preoccupation with calorie counting

- Irritability, anxiety or depression

- Eating in secret

Eating Disorders Stats and Info

If you think you suffer from an eating disorder, you're not alone. In fact, it's estimated that 5 to 20 percent of college females and 1 to 7 percent of college males have eating disorders. Additionally, according to the National Association of Anorexia Nervosa:

- At least 30 million people in the United States – of all ages and genders – suffer from an eating disorder.

- At least one person dies almost hourly as a direct result of an eating disorder.

- 16 percent of transgender college students report having an eating disorder.

- 1 in every 5 anorexia-related deaths is caused by suicide.

- Eating disorders have the highest mortality rate of any mental illness.

Getting Help

Eating disorders usually aren't solitary conditions. Most teens who suffer from an eating disorder are also suffering from other mental or psychiatric disorders or issues (remember Jackie?). Eating disorders may serve as a coping mechanism for the underlying issue – perfectionism, anxiety, depression, PTSD or any number of other issues. When eating disorders go untreated, they become worse and can lead to lifelong health problems or even death. If you or someone you know has an eating disorder, it's time to get help – tell an adult you trust immediately.

Ask the Question

Like so many suffering from depression, Jackie might have had a different story if someone, at some point, had asked the right question. If you think someone is depressed, you can begin a conversation with them by asking these three simple words:

R U OK?

When you take a brave step to start a conversation with those three words, you'll open the door to encourage them to get the help they need. Believe it or not, teens who are depressed or considering suicide are usually willing to talk if someone asks them if they are okay out of genuine concern and care.

When someone is depressed, he or she is not able to see the answers or solutions to problems clearly. That's when speaking with a trusted friend or relative can help the person recognize or identify healthy ways out of a bad situation. Sometimes finding that light in the tunnel starts with a simple conversation.

When a friend or family member opens up to you, that takes courage and trust. But that trust does not – and should not – swear you to silence. If the topic of suicide arises, whatever you do, whatever you think, whatever you say, this is one time to not keep secrets.

In fact, if your friend or classmate swears you to secrecy, get them help immediately; tell an adult you trust as soon as possible!

What's Going on in Your Brain?

When we talk about depression and its effect on the brain, it's important to also discuss the difference between a *teen's* brain and that of a healthy adult.

Have you ever done something or said something and later thought, "What was I thinking?"

There's a logical explanation for that (even though in hindsight, the action might seem anything but logical). Your brain actually develops from the back to the front. The first part of development includes the cerebellum, amygdala and the nucleus accumbens. These structures control your physical activity, emotion and motivation.

The front part of your brain is the last to develop. This includes the prefrontal cortex. This portion of your brain controls reasoning and impulse. While you might feel like an adult, in reality your brain takes about 25 years to fully mature and develop. In your adolescence, you'll experience a huge burst of development, and this could explain a lot of unpredictable and risky behaviors. The immaturity of the brain could help explain why you may act first and think later at times.

Often, teenagers act with impulsivity – even recklessness. This is particularly true if their judgment is further clouded by depression or another mental illness. For example, a teen might impulsively hit or lash out at a peer simply because of something negative he or she said. A more extreme example is speeding or reckless driving.

As your brain is developing, it's actually more susceptible to damage. This is particularly true when you use alcohol and/or drugs, which can have lasting, harmful effects on your brain. (Keep reading for more information on that.)

The bottom line is your brain is a work in progress; how you feel now isn't indicative of how you'll feel tomorrow or in ten years. If you're suffering from depression or another mental health condition, these confusing, impulsive or even reckless thoughts are likely magnified. That's why it's so important for you to understand that there is hope. You're not alone, and there are people who understand how you feel and, more importantly, *why* you feel that way.

Sofia's Story

When my sister, Sofia, completed suicide, no one saw it coming. Being five years older, I was in college the year Sofia decided to take her life. My parents, her school counselors, friends and teachers were unaware of the pain my sister was suffering from on a daily basis. Unfortunately, when she decided she couldn't take anymore, no one was there to stop her.

Two years before Sofia's suicide, my family moved from a small town in Northern California to a large suburb of Los Angeles. Sofia was 15, a freshman in high school, and had always had a good group of friends. She was pretty and popular in our hometown. When she started school after our move, she struggled to fit in. She was still friendly and pretty, but her grade was filled with cliques of girls who were unwilling to befriend new girls. Even worse, they wanted to make sure Sofia knew she didn't belong.

Since she was 4 or 5, Sofia wore glasses to help her see far away. Suddenly, her glasses were a target for abuse. The girls near her locker called her a nerd and said she was even uglier without the glasses than she was with them. In P.E. class, another group of girls made fun of Sofia because of her small breasts and boyish figure. They teased her constantly, telling her she should change in the boy's locker room.

Online, the bullying was even worse. Sofia's classmates used anonymous or hidden social media accounts to terrorize her. Classmates would take photos of her in the locker room and post them online. Sometimes, she'd receive threatening messages telling her if she didn't kill herself someone else would do her a favor and do it for her.

My little sister was absolutely miserable. Unfortunately, we didn't know it. While she gradually became more and more withdrawn, she didn't speak of the bullying to me or our parents. She spent more time in her room, sleeping whenever possible. Sofia had always been a smart, successful student. Suddenly, she was pulling C's and incompletes in her favorite classes. After her death, we discovered Sofia's ankles bore dozens of scars that appeared to be self-inflicted cuts.

When Sofia no longer wanted to go to school, our parents thought she was going through a phase of teenage angst. They told her she needed to try to make friends and work harder on her grades. Inside, Sofia was dying, but we weren't able to give her the help she so desperately needed. If Sofia had had a close friend in her school, perhaps he or she would have told us what was going on – or told anyone. But instead, Sofia was completely alone.

One day she decided she couldn't take it anymore. She wrote a letter to me and one to our parents before she hanged herself in her bedroom. The letters simply said that she loved us and was sorry. It wasn't until later we discovered what was happening to her at school and online.

The most devastating part of Sofia's death is that it didn't need to happen. There are so many people that could have or would have helped her. But Sofia felt so isolated and alone she couldn't go to any of us. And we failed to see the warning signs that now seem so obvious. If there's one thing I hope can come of her death, it's that anyone reading this takes the risk factors and warning signs of suicide seriously. And that they never, ever engage in bullying another person. Those words, threats and insults have more power than you think. They do more than hurt; they can kill.

Bullying

Sticks and stones can break your bones… and words can absolutely destroy. For teens today, bullying is not only a schoolyard game; it can be a potentially life-threatening phenomenon. That's because bullying is quickly becoming one of the biggest factors linked to teen suicide. In fact, teens who are bullied are seven to nine times more likely to consider suicide than those who are not.

What is bullying?

Generally speaking, bullying refers to unsolicited harassment and aggression. Bullying involves violence – either physical or psychological – aimed at a person or group of people. While you may occasionally argue or fight with a friend or peer, bullying is underscored by a more insidious intent. In a nutshell, a bully is trying to inflict pain and suffering on another person (or several people), and does so strategically. Bullying takes many forms, but can include insults, name-calling, pushing, shoving, hitting, threatening and public embarrassment. Bullying is usually repetitive, and because of this, it can quickly become psychologically damaging. Bullies often feel they have superiority over their victim, whether that's due to physical appearance, popularity, age, intelligence, race, sex, ethnicity or socioeconomic status. Bullies use this superiority to gain power over their victims, whether physically or psychologically.

Cyberbullying

Today, much of our lives occur online. And unfortunately, because of that, bullying also takes place online. Cyberbullying is the term used to describe bullying that happens via social media, text messages or other forms of digital communication. In Sofia's case, she received anonymous threats online, and bullies used social media to publically humiliate her by posting embarrassing and inappropriate photos. Cyberbullying isn't about a one-time insult on social media. As with in-person bullying, cyberbullying is intentional and repetitive in nature. Victims of bullying have a relationship with their aggressor, although it's not a healthy one. Cyberbullying can be particularly harmful because bullies are often strategic in covering their tracks, making it easier for them to bully their victims indefinitely.

Bullying and Suicide

Often, parents and other adults consider bullying just part of growing up. But bullying can have devastating effects on its victims. As mentioned before, victims of bullying are much more likely to attempt or complete suicide than those who are not bullied. According to JAMA Pediatrics, peer victimization and bullying causes higher rates of suicide, with cyberbullying specifically leading to more thoughts of suicide (more so than traditional bullying).

Bullying Statistics

- 69 percent of teens own their own cell phone, computer and use social media.

- 42 percent of teens report they've been victims of online bullying.

- Girls ages 14 to 16 send an average of 100 text messages a day, double the rate for adults.

- 20 percent of teens who are bullied think about suicide.

- Only one in five cyberbullying incidents is reported.

- 81 percent of teens consider cyberbullying easier to get away with than traditional bullying.

- As many as one in four school-aged children and teens are bullied on a regular basis.

- 35 percent of teens report they've been threatened online.

- 58 percent of children and teens report they've had something mean said about them online.

Bullying Risk Factors

While bullying can happen to anyone, it is specifically more common for teens and children who:

- Are overweight or underweight

- Are new students (remember Sofia's story?)

- Are poor or in a lower socioeconomic class

- Who suffer from depression or anxiety

- Are unpopular

- Are or are suspected to be LGBTQ

- Have low self-esteem

- Have few friends

- Do not get along well with others

Bullying Warning Signs - Victims

As you might remember from Sofia's story, sometimes parents, siblings and other loved ones fail to notice the warning signs for bullying (and suicide). Sofia exhibited many of the warning signs for bullying, but unfortunately her parents mistook this for teenage moodiness. Here are some of the common warning signs that a peer, child or loved one is being bullied:

- Unexplained bruises or injuries

- Difficulty sleeping

- Frequent illness (stomachachcs, headaches, feeling unwell)

- Skipping meals (especially lunches at school)

- Declining grades or academic performance

- The desire to stay home from school (or withdraw altogether)

- Lost or destroyed possessions, like clothes, shoes, electronics, etc.

- Loneliness/lack of friends

- Self-injury, like cutting, burning and hitting

Bullying Warning Signs – Aggressor

No one wants to believe their son/daughter/friend/loved one is a bully, but unfortunately, children and teens *do* bully. Often, children and teens who bully have been bullied themselves at some point in their lives, or have been abused in some way. It's even possible that a teen who is bullying is also being bulled by someone else. Here are some common signs that a teen you know is bullying:

- Friendships with other teens known to bully

- Frequently getting into physical fights

- Acts of aggression at home or school

- An increase in disciplinary action in school (detention/suspension)

- Frequently blaming others for problems and actions

- Preoccupied about his or her reputation or popularity

Get Help

Unfortunately, many victims of bullying feel helpless and alone. These feelings make it difficult for a victim to seek help. Additionally, bullying is a play for power, and victims often fear that speaking up would result in severe backlash – either from the bully or his or her peers. The goal of bullying is humiliation, and many teens and kids try to mitigate the humiliation by pretending everything is fine.

The thing is, it's not. Bullying can lead to insecurity, low self-esteem, depression, anxiety and thoughts of suicide. Talking to an adult you trust is the only way you can help the situation. This isn't about tattling; it's about saving a life, either yours or someone you love.

Symptoms of Depression

Do you or does someone you know relate to any of these symptoms of depression?

- loss of interest in previously fun activities

- conflict/fights with family or friends

- low self-esteem

- complaints of pains, including headaches, stomachaches, low back pain or fatigue

- difficulty concentrating, making decisions or remembering things

- excessive or inappropriate guilt

- irresponsible behavior: skipping school, class tardiness, forgetfulness

- loss of interest in food or compulsive overeating

- preoccupation with death, dying and suicide

- rebellious behavior

- sadness, anxiety or feelings of hopelessness

- staying awake at night and sleeping during the day

- sudden drop in grades

- use of alcohol or drugs

- promiscuous sexual activity

- withdrawal from friends and family

- crying for no apparent reason

- feelings of anger, even over small things

- fixation on past failures, self-blame or self-criticism

- feeling that life and the future are grim and bleak

You are Not Alone

Take the Quiz.

Fifteen million kids in the U.S. have parents with depression.

Those 15 million kids are at greater risk of developing depression simply because their parents have it. The faster you recognize the symptoms of depression, the faster you or a loved one can get treatment.

Are you at risk for depression?

Take the quiz

Do you currently live with a family member who suffers from depression?

Whether the cause is environmental or genetic, studies have shown that living with a mother or father who has depression increases your own risk of developing the condition. Whether your depressed family member lives with you or is simply a blood relative, you may be at risk.

Does life feel pointless?

You may occasionally feel hopeless as you navigate your way through school. But if this hopeless feeling persists day after day and affects your daily behavior, it could be a sign of depression.

Do you find it impossible to concentrate?

If you have a tough time concentrating even when you're reading or watching something you love, depression could be the reason.

Have you withdrawn from your friends and family?

Sure, it's cool to do your own thing and be independent, but you should also balance that with a healthy amount of social bonding time with your friends and family. Do you find yourself turning down opportunities to be with others in order to be alone? Depression could be to blame.

Have you noticed a sudden change in your weight?

Extreme weight loss or gain can be a symptom of depression. If you've lost your appetite or find yourself seeking comfort in food, your brain may be experiencing a change in chemistry as a result of depression.

Do you have insomnia or do you sleep too much?

Look, you're a teenager. You need your sleep and often you don't get enough. But if you go through any long periods of sleeplessness or sleeping too much, depression may be the reason.

Do you have physical pain that won't go away?

Depression isn't just about emotional pain. If you have physical pain that persists and a medical professional has not found a reason for it, it could be depression causing a chemical imbalance in your brain that makes you perceive pain differently.

Have your grades dropped? Have you stopped participating in extracurricular activities?

Depression has two best friends: apathy and lack of energy. These can combine to affect your performance in school and your extracurricular activities. If you find your passion for activities you once loved fading away, depression could be the source.

Have you thought of suicide?

If your answer is "yes," you're not alone. One thing a professional will ask you – if you're thinking about suicide – is to hold off doing anything until you get treatment. With counseling and possible medical treatment, you will probably begin to feel better and thoughts of suicide will disappear. When you're suffering from depression, the idea of feeling better might be difficult to imagine. This is the time to practice trust and courage. There are support resources available to help you get back to your old self.

What to Say and What Not to Say

So, what can you do if a friend of yours is depressed?

In addition to beginning the conversation by asking "R U OK?" you can support a depressed friend by:

- letting them know you care

- being willing to listen

- inviting them to join you in daily activities

- acknowledging them for small accomplishments

- offering reassurance and kindness

- showing them you are on their side

Today, we live – and communicate – from text message to text message. This can actually be a great tool in getting through to someone who doesn't want to "listen" or who isn't around to talk. Sometimes, a little note of love and understanding sent in a simple text can go a long way.

What to Say

These are examples of little messages that go a long way. You can use them as inspiration and make them your own so they feel natural coming from you. You should also feel free to add your own positive emojis or emoticons to enforce the words, but *do be sure to* use _your actual words_ and not only fun pictures. Sometimes it's hard to put feelings and thoughts into words, but language is far more powerful, impactful and helpful, particularly to someone going through a very rough time.

I'm always here for you, even when times are bad.

I love you for who you are.

I'm on your side.

We're a team.

You are important to me.

I can't imagine how hard this is for you, but I want to help in any way I can.

You are not alone.

You are a sensitive person and care so much for others.

This is an illness, and it's nothing to be ashamed of. It can happen to any-one.

I understand that you find difficulty in doing everything, but if you lean on me, we'll make it.

I'm a good listener, so pour out your feelings.

Is there anything I can do?

You make my life better just by being in it.

I will always have your back.

Don't let darkness steal the beautiful person inside.

You are never a burden.

I'm not going anywhere.

I'm beginning to understand how loud silence can be. Forgive me for not standing still enough to hear yours. I'm listening.

What Not to Say

Take your mind off of it and just go and have fun.

There are a lot of people who have it worse than you do.

Stop your pity party.

Just get out and do something.

It's all in your head.

You'll be fine after a good night's sleep.

Stop playing the victim and grow up already. You'll get over it.

You have no reason to be anything but happy.

Things really aren't that bad.

Just smile.

You don't look depressed.

You're doing this to attract attention.

I've had things a lot tougher than you.

No one ever said life was fair.

You're bringing this on yourself.

You're always so negative.

What to Do

Remember that cartoon character that has a dark rain cloud following him wherever he goes, all the time? The rest of the world seems sunny and fine, but that character can't escape the nonstop pouring rain.

That's what depression is like. It's all consuming. But unlike the cartoon, there's nothing funny about it.

The thing is, even the most severe depression is treatable. There is help and there are resources. Learning about your depression treatment options will help you to decide what approach is right for you. From therapy to different lifestyle changes, there are many effective treatments that can help you overcome depression and reclaim your life.

You may be currently hanging with depression's best buds: apathy and lack of energy. Be patient with yourself and don't give yourself a hard time. Celebrate each accomplishment. Take small steps, because small steps quickly add up. If you continue to take positive steps each day, you will find that you will feel better – slowly but surely.

There are changes you can make in your own life to support your journey out of depression:

Move every day. When you're depressed, just climbing out of bed can seem utterly impossible, let alone working out. But exercise is a powerful depression-fighter and one of the most important tools for relieving depression symptoms. Exercise increases your body temperature, which helps produce a feeling of warmth and releases endorphins, the feel-good chemicals in your brain that help improve your mood. Exercise also helps prevent relapse once you're well. Any type of movement can make a difference, so find something you enjoy so you'll stick with it. It can be skateboarding, walking the dog, dancing. Even a 10-minute walk can improve your mood. Work your way up to at least 30 minutes of exercise per day. Don't be afraid to ask a friend or family member to join you, as it can help to have another person with you for support and encouragement.

Eat well. There's a reason the expression "you are what you eat" **exists.** Caffeine and alcohol affect your brain and mood, while foods containing preservatives, trans fat or hormones can make you feel worse. Cutting back on junk food and replacing it with nutritious snacks can positively impact how you feel. Ask your parents to get rid of unhealthy temptations in your home to support your change in habit; if the bad food items aren't physically in your house, you won't eat them because they aren't as easily accessible. Cut out sugar and refined carbohydrates found in foods like baked goods, french fries and pasta, as these can make your mood and energy crash. Eating healthy meals or snacks every three to four hours can also keep your blood sugar stable and prevent you from feeling slow and unmotivated. A Vitamin B deficiency can trigger depression, so eat more citrus fruit, leafy greens, beans, salmon and eggs.

Socialize. When you're depressed, it's way easier to just shut everyone out, but being around other people will absolutely make you feel better. Isolation leads to loneliness, which can increase your depression level. Stay connected with your friends. Don't be shy about asking friends and family to reach out to you via text message and phone calls and to include you in social plans. In fact, ask them to persist even when you have the urge to refuse invitations. Remember, no one can go it alone and now is the time when you need friends who will listen and lend their support. You may be surprised at how much better you feel once you're out having a good time. Staying engaged and busy can keep your mind active and is a better alternative than sitting at home. You will gradually feel more upbeat and energized as you make time for activities and people you truly enjoy.

Get out in the sunlight. Lack of sunlight can make depression worse. Get outside; take a short walk or eat lunch on a park bench. Aim for at least 15 minutes of sunlight a day to boost your mood.

Support others. You can get a big mood boost from providing support to others in big or small ways, and doing this will also briefly shift your attention to something beyond your own troubles. Volunteer, be an ear for a friend, go to a friend's play or concert or game, or do something nice for a family member or neighbor.

Don't be afraid to vent. The process of letting out your pent-up feelings and emotions is a healthy way to help combat your depression. I'm not talking about screaming into a pillow (though if you want to do that, go right ahead). Start with "I feel" and use your words to let it all out to a friend, family member, teacher, therapist or other adult. Giving a voice to these emotions can actually help you identify some of the negative feelings associated with your depression and is an important step in your treatment.

Be committed to getting good sleep. The ideal amount of sleep is usually eight hours or more each night. And for teenagers, it can be another hour or two on top of that. When you're sleep-deprived, being optimistic and making good decisions is even more challenging. When you're overtired, you may find yourself exaggerating small stressors because your coping skills have been compromised.

Stay away from drugs and alcohol. When you don't like how you feel or act, you may experiment with alcohol or drugs in an effort to self-medicate and feel better. But drugs and alcohol usually just make a bad situation even worse.

Focus on having fun. Focus on fun – make it a primary daily goal for yourself and don't let your depression get in your way. Pleasurable activities raise the dopamine levels in your brain, which work to combat your depression.

Learn how to relax. A daily relaxation practice can help relieve depression, reduce stress and boost feelings of joy and wellbeing. Different people will respond differently to relaxation techniques such as yoga, deep breathing or mediation. There are meditation apps, books and YouTube videos. You can do yoga videos online or search for classes in your area. Some yoga studios offer donation-based classes, or pay what you can. You can experiment and see what works best for you.

Think. Depression puts a negative spin on everything in your life, especially the way you see yourself and how you see your future. You may feel like bad things continue to happen and there's not much you can do about it. These thoughts can become overwhelming, playing on a constant loop in your mind. This is the depression talking. Often times these thoughts are part of a lifelong pattern of thinking that's become so automatic to you that you're not even completely aware you're doing it. Try challenging your thinking. Stand up to it, asking "Is this thought true?" "What would I tell a friend who had this thought?" "Is there another way of looking at the situation or another explanation?" "How would I look at the situation if I didn't have depression?" You may surprise yourself by developing a more balanced perspective if you take a step back and try to look at your own thoughts as an objective observer.

Seek professional treatment. Self-help strategies are tools that can decrease your depression symptoms and empower you to feel better, yet it is important to know that they are only a supplement to professional treatment and not a replacement. Talking with a professional therapist is a great way to work toward feeling that you have more control over your life and to get you back on your road to recovery.

Work with a professional while using these tips on a daily basis, and you can speed your recovery and prevent depression from returning in the future.

Kaley's Story

I grew up in Pennsylvania with divorced parents who lived in different states. As a single mom, my mother worked full time, and after school I usually ended up at my uncle's house. Because he lived just a few blocks away and worked nights, he was almost always home in the afternoon. When I was 11 or so, my uncle began molesting me, and as a child with little understanding of what was happening and a mother who was always under a lot of stress, I didn't tell anyone about the abuse. It went on for several years; usually it happened only when my uncle was angry or drunk.

Rather than telling anyone about what was happening, I became very quiet, shy and withdrawn. I thought that if I could make my mother happy and my uncle happy, the abuse would stop, but it continued despite how I acted or what I did. After a few years, my mother got a new job in another town and we moved away. By this time I was a teenager, and my mom still had no idea what had happened so many times at my uncle's house.

Even after I moved and the abuse stopped, I felt very isolated and alone. I would go over and over the events in my head and think about all the things I could have done differently that might have made it stop – or prevented it altogether. At times like these I would find myself digging my fingernails into my skin so hard I sometimes bled. It was like I was punishing myself for all the actions I didn't take when I could have.

I tried to make friends, but I always felt isolated and different and never knew quite what to say. The loneliness made me depressed, and in school I was always wary and suspicious of adults – particularly male adults – and couldn't bring myself to open up to anyone.

One day when I was 15, I sat alone in my bedroom thinking about the abuse. I had a paper clip in my hand and slowly straightened it out so I had the point of it against the skin of my forearm. I pressed it into my skin hard, scraping it until I saw a small path of blood. It should have hurt, but I just felt relief. I focused on the stinging in my skin rather than all the thoughts running through my mind, and I felt better than I had in so long.

Not long after, I walked into a hardware store after school and bought a package of razor blades. I kept these hidden in my desk at home, and when the thoughts and memories were too much for me to bear, I'd make a cut on my forearm. Sometimes the cuts were shallow scratches, sometimes deeper. Once I worried I might need stitches, but I didn't want anyone to find out about what I was doing.

I stopped wearing tank tops and even short sleeves. Even in the summer heat, I wore long-sleeve shirts to make sure no one saw my arms. One day when I was just out of the shower, my mother caught a glimpse of a fresh cut and forced me to show her my arms. She asked why I would do this to myself and I couldn't answer. I didn't *know* why I did it. I just knew that it made me feel better.

My mom arranged for me to talk to a counselor. After several very quiet sessions, I finally told the counselor about the abuse. That was when she explained to *me* why I was cutting. I had experienced sexual abuse and continued to experience post-traumatic stress (PTSD) from those events.

Once I opened up about the abuse and began taking positive steps toward working through it, I realized that I didn't have the same urge to cut anymore. Of course, there were days – and still are – that were overwhelming, and all those feelings of guilt, shame, isolation and pain would come flooding back. At those times, I sometimes found myself imagining how it would feel to cut again. Often this happened after an event or situation that reminded me of the time in my life I was being abused.

Working with a counselor, I was able to address the root cause of my cutting and the reason for my post-traumatic stress. Through her help, I became healthy enough to make new friends, and eventually I graduated from college and now have a successful, professional career. The scars of my past are still visible – literally – and I'm often still self-conscious of them. But those who are closest to me know what they're from and why they're there. To say that I'm the same person I was before I experienced the abuse would be untrue, but I'm a happy, healthy adult and have been able to make and maintain healthy relationships.

Self-harm isn't something I ever planned to do, or really even thought about. But for me, it offered an outlet when I didn't know where to turn. I hope that teens reading this know that there are so many other outlets out there – your teachers, counselors and parents, just to name a few. Even a close friend might be the person who helps you make a positive change. You're not alone, so please don't ever think there's nowhere else to turn.

Self-Harm

Everyone deals with emotions differently. You might be someone who gets angry and lashes out at others when you feel stressed out, disappointed or embarrassed. Or you could become withdrawn and isolated when you feel worried or fearful. For some – particularly teens – self-harm (also called self-injury) is a coping mechanism for overwhelming feelings and emotions.

So what is self-harm? In short, it's the act of hurting yourself in order to cope with emotions that seem too much to bear. If you've never felt the urge to self-harm, or if you've never had experience with someone who has, you might think this sounds a bit like suicide – after all, that's the ultimate self-harm, right? Self-injury is actually a totally different animal. It's not about suicide – *usually*. It's about finding an outlet for pain, shame, guilt or other emotions that simply seem too great to bear. That said, one of the dangers of self-harm is that accidental death *can* occur, and we'll get to that later.

Remember Kaley from the story you just read? Like many cutters, she didn't understand why she was doing what she was doing. She simply knew that it made her feel better. For many, self-injury provides an emotional release when they feel they have no other outlet. For others, the injury serves as an interruption from the numbness or nothingness (often caused by depression) they feel on a daily basis. Sometimes, self-injury can be a subtle

– even subconscious – cry for help, while in others it could be a way in which to feel a sense of control when they feel everything else is *out* of control.

Types of Self-Harm

Not everyone who practices self-harm does so in the same manner. Cutting is a common form of self-injury, but burning, pulling hair, skin picking, hitting and head-banging are not unheard of. Because self-injury is a coping strategy and not a manipulation tactic, those who practice it are often secretive about what they're doing. That means it can be even harder for them to get the help they need.

Risks of Self-Harm

You already know that self-injury is a coping mechanism. But that doesn't make it a healthy one. Self-injury is a risky behavior because, well, you're *injuring* yourself. Firstly, there's always the chance that you'll cut too deep, hit too hard, or cause yourself a serious infection or permanent injury. Secondly, self-injury is an unhealthy way to express feelings, thoughts, fears and experiences. Aside from the physical effects of the injury – like bruises, scars, nerve damage, broken bones, hair loss and other physical ailments – self-injury also results in serious psychological effects. People who practice self-injury often experience feelings of shame and guilt over their behavior, leading to lower self-esteem and depression. Self-injury can be addictive and, like many addictions, can become worse and worse until the behavior is a serious health risk.

Signs and Symptoms of Self-Injury

People who practice self-harm are usually pretty secretive about the behavior. That means it can be tough to spot the warning signs in your friends or loved ones. Some of the most common signs and symptoms of self-harm include:

- Scars that can't be explained

- Bald spots (where the person has pulled out hair)

- Burns or marks on the skin

- Keeping sharp objects – likes pocket knives or razor blades – around

- Spending a lot of time alone

- Wearing long-sleeved clothing or long pants even on warm days

- Avoiding talking about feelings or expressing emotions

Risk Factors

So why do some teens self-harm while others don't? According to Teen Help, one-third to one-half of U.S. adolescents have engaged in some kind of self-injury, and one in every 200 girls aged 13 to 19 cut themselves regularly. Additionally, some teens might be at greater risk than others for self-injury. A few of these risk factors include but are not limited to:

- A history of physical or sexual abuse

- Age: pre-adolescents and teens are more likely to hurt themselves than other age groups

- Sex: adolescent girls are the most common demographic for self-injury

- A family history of self-injury

- Mental illness, including depression and anxiety

- Alcohol and substance abuse

- A history of PTSD

So let's go back to Kaley. Kaley was at serious risk for self-injury for several reasons. Not only was she an adolescent female, but she also had a history of sexual abuse. Because of that abuse, Kaley suffered from post-traumatic stress disorder (PTSD) and depression. Kaley used self-injury as an outlet for her emotions, which due to her experiences were totally overwhelming.

So what changed? The thing about self-harm is that it usually masks the real issue. Like drugs and alcohol, self-injury might offer temporary relief or distraction, but it actually exacerbates the underlying problems. Kaley only began to feel better when she confronted the main cause of her self-injury, PTSD and depression: her experience with sexual abuse.

Self-Injury Stats and Info

- Each year, 1 in 5 females and 1 in 7 males engages in self-harm.

- 90 percent of people who self-harm began doing so in their teenage or pre-adolescent years.

- The most common methods of self-injury are cutting (70-90 percent), head banging or hitting (21-44 percent) and burning (15-35 percent).

- Self-injury is usually a symptom of other mental illnesses, like borderline personality disorder, bipolar, major depression and anxiety disorders.

- 17 percent of adolescents have engaged in non-suicidal self-injury at least once.

What to do

If you know someone who practices self-harm (or if you do yourself), the most important thing for you to know is this: it's not going to solve your problems. Only addressing the underlying reasons for self-injury will help you find healthy ways to cope. The best way to help a friend who self-injures is to make sure you're not adding to their shame. Encourage them to tell a responsible adult – a relative, teacher or counselor – and get the help they need. This isn't the time to keep secrets; self-injury is serious and can even be fatal when it's taken too far. The most important thing for you or your friend to know is that there's someone out there who cares enough to help you through it.

Post-traumatic Stress Disorder

When you hear the term "post-traumatic stress disorder," what comes to mind? If you're like me, you might think about soldiers at war, witnessing a horrific, violent event or something like that. Of course, those are valid – and common – causes of PTSD, but did you know that many kids and teens suffer from PTSD? Many adolescents have experienced significantly traumatic events or bouts of acute stress. Those events or feelings of fear, stress and pain can affect you for a long, long time – particularly if you suffer from PTSD.

What is PTSD?

So what is post-traumatic stress disorder? When you encounter a scary situation, your brain experiences a "fight or flight" response which basically determines how you (and your body) will react to the situation: you'll either defend yourself or you'll avoid it. This response is natural and aimed at helping you stay out of harm's way. Unfortunately, people with PTSD continue to feel that fight-or-flight response even when there's no actual danger present.

But here's the thing. Not every teen with PTSD has experienced a horrific event, and not every person who *has* experienced trauma suffers from PTSD. Other situations – like a sudden loss of a loved one, neglect or abuse – can cause PTSD for months or even years after the trauma ends. What's more, some teens with PTSD will suffer for a matter of months, while others experience a chronic and even lifelong condition. That's why it's so important to seek the help of a professional.

Signs of PTSD

PTSD is a disorder fueled by memories. The symptoms of PTSD are all about how your mind and body react to or recall those memories. These symptoms include:

- Nightmares

- Flashbacks

- Detachments

- Depression

- Avoiding situations that trigger memories of the event

- Irritability or emotional outbursts

- Insomnia

- Headaches

- Anxiety about danger

- Inability to get your mind off the event(s)

Usually, symptoms of PTSD develop within about three months of the trauma or event, but like any mental disorder, every case is different. Sometimes PTSD doesn't occur until years after the trauma. While any stressful or traumatic situation could result in PTSD, there are several reasons one person might be at greater risk than another.

Risk Factors

Risk factors of PTSD include but are not limited to:

- History of abuse (physical, psychological or sexual)

- Neglect

- Drug and alcohol abuse

- Lack of social support

- Survivors of traumatic events (car accidents, terror attacks, natural disasters, etc.)

- Veterans or witnesses of war

- Gender (females are more likely to develop PTSD)

Of course, not everyone with the textbook risk factors suffers from PTSD. If you read through Kaley's story again, you'd see that she had a history of sexual abuse and a lack of social support. These factors played a role in Kaley's development of PTSD.

PTSD Stats and Info

According to the National Center for PTSD:

- Neglect is the leading cause of PTSD in children and young adults (65 percent).

- Other causes of PTSD in children and teens include physical abuse (18 percent), sexual abuse (10 percent) and psychological abuse (7 percent).

- 3 million to 10 million children witness family violence each year, with about 40 to 60 percent of those cases involving child abuse.

- 15 to 43 percent of girls and 14 to 43 percent of boys experience at least one trauma. Of those, 3 to 15 percent of girls and 1 to 6 percent of boys develop PTSD.

- Teens are more likely than younger children or adults to show impulsive or aggressive behaviors in response to PTSD.

What to Do

Living with PTSD isn't something any teen should have to experience. Fortunately, as with other mental disorders, there's help available for you when you need it. Of course, the best thing to do anytime you fear you might have a mental illness or disorder is to talk to a health care professional, but I understand that may not be a totally comfortable situation for you. First and foremost, talk to someone you trust, preferably an adult. Your friends can be a great support system, but an adult is more likely to have the resources and know-how to help you get the help you really need. If you don't think you can talk to your parents about PTSD, try a school counselor, family doctor, a clergy member at your church, a teacher or even a close family friend you trust.

Secondly, don't wait. Symptoms of PTSD tend to get worse without treatment, not better. Dealing with these symptoms now can help you avoid living through months or even years of continued trauma and stress.

Remember, like depression, PTSD is *treatable*. There's hope for you – just as there was for Kaley. That first step is difficult but critical in helping you become your happiest, healthiest self.

Why Suicide Happens

Did you know that most teens, after making a suicide attempt, say that they did it because they were trying to escape from a situation that seemed impossible to deal with or to get relief from bad thoughts or feelings?

They didn't want to die as much as they wanted to escape what was going on. And at that particular moment, dying seemed like the only way out.

Some people who end their lives or attempt suicide might be trying to escape feelings of rejection, hurt or loss.

Others feel angry, ashamed or guilty about something (remember Jackie's story?)

Some may be worried about disappointing friends or family.

Others feel unwanted, unloved, bullied, abused or a burden to others.

All of us feel overwhelmed by difficult situations and emotions at times. But most of us get through it or can find a way to carry on with determination and hope.

So why does one person try suicide when another in a similar situation does not?

Why are some of us more resilient than others?

What makes a person unable to see another way out of a bad situation besides ending his or her life?

The answer to these questions is that most people who complete suicide have *depression*.

Teen Suicide Myths

Do the following instructions sound familiar? Your parents have probably said these statements before, and all this stuff may seem obvious to you (and that's great if it does):

"Don't meet strangers online."

"Don't stay out after dark."

"Please don't text and drive."

"Don't do drugs."

But guess what? Most parents never talk about suicide. Let's face it – suicide is really sad, and it's uncomfortable. A lot of people don't know what to say or how to approach the topic of suicide, so instead they say or do nothing at all. But did you know that as a teenager, you are statistically more at risk of dying from suicide than cancer, the flu, lung disease, heart disease, AIDS, pneumonia and birth defects *combined*?

This tells us that it's time to start the conversation. And that conversation begins with *you*.

Here are some common myths about teen suicide:

Teens who threaten to complete suicide are just looking for attention.

This is not true. A teen talking about suicide should be taken seriously. Remember what I already said about keeping secrets? If you or someone you know has mentioned suicide, tell an adult you trust immediately.

Asking teens if they have had thoughts about suicide increases their risk.

This is not true. Parents sometimes fear that bringing up the subject of suicide will somehow plant the seed to complete the act when, in fact, the opposite is true. Bringing painful subjects like suicidal thoughts to light creates a safe space and a sense of relief for the individual having those thoughts since he or she realizes someone cares and there is help available.

Teens who aren't successful in completing suicide weren't serious.

This is not true. A teen who attempts suicide is trying to end his or her pain and suffering and is at a much higher risk of trying again. Second attempts at suicide are more likely to be lethal. Lethal is *permanent.*

Teens who complete suicide always act sad beforehand.

This is not true. A teen who completes suicide may appear irritable or withdrawn and also happy at times. Suicide can actually be a rather sudden response to a major stressful event.

Teens who complete suicide spend a lot of time planning it.

This is not always true. Suicide may be planned, but it could also be a completely impulsive act. Whether it is planned or impulsive, suicide may feel like the best way to escape pain.

Suicide among teens is rare.

This is false. Suicide is the second leading cause of death among teenagers. Teens who struggle with mental health issues like depression as well as those who abuse drugs and alcohol are at a higher risk of taking their own life.

Suicide is selfish.

That is an opinion — a judgment, but it's not what a suicidal person thinks. When someone is severely depressed, he or she thinks their family and the world would be better off without him or her. They feel as though they are a total failure and their life has no point or does not matter.

Teens who complete suicide must have wanted to die.

This is not true. Individuals who complete suicide want to end their pain. Think about when you were a child and you scraped your knee and cried and screamed your head off. You wanted comfort, something to take the physical pain away. Someone who is contemplating suicide wants to end his or her emotional pain and sees dying as the only way to accomplish that.

If you try to protect someone by taking away his method, he'll just find another way to kill himself.

This is not true. A study tracking 515 people who were saved before they jumped from the Golden Gate Bridge found that 90 percent were alive or had died from natural causes decades later. Intervention can lead to help and save lives.

People don't copycat.

This is not true. Copycat is when someone completes suicide one way, it is reported in the news extensively, and then there are reports of other people completing suicide in the same way. Copycatting is a real problem and dozens of studies have shown that pervasive coverage or reporting specific details can pave the way for copycats.

Suicidal thoughts are rare.

This is not true because suicidal thoughts run on a spectrum. *Fleeting* thoughts of suicide are fairly common. However, if these thoughts happen frequently, particularly if you're struggling through a hard time, it could be that your brain is asking you for help. The worrisome, high end of the suicide spectrum is when someone makes a specific plan involving when, where and how to kill themselves.

Suicide Risk Factors, Warning Signs, Stats and Info

Some of the risk factors for suicide may be inherited, such as a family history of suicide. Others, such as physical illnesses, may also be out of your control. It is important to recognize risk factors for suicide early and act to change those you can control so you can save your life or possibly the life of a close friend or family member.

Suicide risk factors include but are not limited to:

- previous suicide attempt(s)

- psychological disorders, especially depression and other mood disorders, schizophrenia, anorexia, social anxiety

- substance abuse

- history of abuse (physical, psychological or sexual)

- family history of suicide

- feelings of hopelessness

- physical illness

- impulsive or aggressive tendencies

- reckless behavior

- financial or social loss

- relationship loss

- isolation

- lack of social support

- easy access to means of suicide

- exposure to others who have completed suicide

- a major traumatic life event (moving, death of a friend or family member, etc.)

We've already discussed that suicide can be an impulsive act. That said, four out of five teen suicide attempts are preceded by clear warning signs that *someone* (or many people) ignored.

Knowing what to look for will sharpen your awareness of yourself and your peers.

Risk factors that can elevate the possibility of suicidal thoughts (include but are not limited to):

- perfectionist personality

- LGBTQ (lesbian, gay, bi-sexual, transgender, questioning)

- learning-disabled youth

- loners

- depressed youth

- youth with low self-esteem

- abused, molested or neglected youth

- parental history of violence, substance abuse or divorce

It is important to know that not all of the signs need to be present for someone to be at risk.

As few as just two or three of the above signs of depression or suicide risk can be a cause for real concern and the need to seek help.

Even good students complete suicide – there is not just one type of person, on the outside or inside, who might be at risk for depression or suicide. Depression does not discriminate.

Let's reiterate that idea: the risk factors can apply to anyone.

Teen suicide warning signs (include but are not limited to):

- disinterest in favorite extracurricular activities

- substance abuse

- behavioral problems

- withdrawing from family and friends

- changes in sleep patterns: sleeping too much or too little

- changes in eating habits: overeating, binging, not eating

- neglecting personal appearance: not showering or messy appearance

- lack of concentration

- declining grades

- deepening depression

- preoccupation with death

- risk-taking or self-destructive behavior

- frequent complaints of boredom

- giving away personal possessions

- saying "goodbye"

Warning signs that there is a suicide plan in place (include but are not limited to):

- Suicidal talk is a big warning sign. Actually saying any of the following is cause for alarm:

  "I'm thinking of killing myself."

  "I want to die."

  "I want you to know in case something happens to me."

  "I won't bother you anymore."

- Giving away favorite belongings, or promising them to friends or family members

- Throwing away important possessions

- Showing signs of extreme cheerfulness following periods of depression

- Creating suicide notes

- Expressing bizarre or disturbing thoughts

The bottom line is that teen suicide warning signs are serious calls for help. It's not cool to play them down or ignore them. They are absolutely a big deal and can literally be a matter of life or death.

Many teenagers share their thoughts and feelings in a desperate attempt to be acknowledged. (Ok, so maybe everyone does this, but it can seem a lot worse when you have a lot of hormones coursing through your body and you're navigating adult issues for the first time.) Anyhow, teens often don't know how to deal with their feelings and problems and are simply looking for someone to help. If these warning signs apply to you or someone you know, respond quickly and seek professional help — you may save a life.

Teen Suicide Stats and Info

Teen suicide isn't just a topic in your health class, it's a very real, very serious problem in the United States. If these U.S. statistics are eye-opening – or shocking – to you, they should be.

- Girls attempt suicide four times more than boys.

- Boys complete suicide four times more than girls.

- Sixty percent of all suicides in the United States make use of a gun.

- Teen suicide is on the rise. For 15- to 24-year-olds, it has increased about 6 percent. For those age 10 to 14, suicides have increased 100 percent.

- About 14.5 percent of high school students have actually made plans for completing suicide.

- About 900,000 youth planned their suicides during episodes of major depression.

- Sixty percent of high school students claim they have thoughts about completing suicide.

- Nine percent of high school students said they have tried killing themselves at least once.

- Stigma surrounding suicide can lead to underreporting, so the estimate of numbers of suicide is most likely higher than statistics indicate.

- Suicide is the second leading cause of death for people ages 10 to 24.

- More teenagers and young adults die from suicide than from cancer, heart disease, AIDS, birth defects, stroke, pneumonia, influenza and chronic lung disease combined.

- Each day in our nation there are, on average, more than 5,240 suicide attempts by young people grades 7 through 12.

- Four out of five teens who attempted suicide gave clear warning signs of what they were about to do.

- Ninety percent of teens who kill themselves have some type of mental health problem such as depression, anxiety, drug or alcohol abuse or a behavioral problem. Common "mood disorders," like bipolar disorder or depression, are actually illnesses of the brain, and they can come on suddenly or may be present on and off during a teen's life.

- There is one age group that really stands out: girls between the ages of 10 and 14. Although they make up a very small portion of the total suicides, the rate in this group has experienced the largest percentage increase, tripling over a 15-year period.

- In any given year, one youth completes suicide for every 25 who attempt it.

Ethan's Story

Ethan is around today because someone noticed the warning signs. As a teenager in New Jersey, Ethan knew what it meant to be a loner. The son of divorced parents, Ethan lived with his dad, grandmother and sister in a middle-class neighborhood. His dad worked long hours and wasn't home much, so Ethan never experienced strict schedules or even vigilant oversight from his family.

Ethan didn't feel like he fit in at school. He had average grades, lived in an average home, but was skinny with a broken-out face and he hated who he was. His self-consciousness, combined with the cruelty of his bullying classmates, made daily life at school incredibly painful. When he expressed these feelings to his dad, he was told so many other kids had it worse; suck it up.

What Ethan really wanted was to disappear.

He thought attending parties might help him do that, especially if he could drink and experiment with drugs. But the drugs didn't offer the escape or self-esteem boost he sought. Instead, he began isolating himself in his room with the one friend he could count on: online video games. The virtual world quickly became Ethan's escape.

Technology soon became Ethan's drug of choice. It was the first thing he thought of when he woke up and the last thing he did before he went to bed. He lied to his father about doing homework when, in fact, he was in front of the screen playing video games. He'd wake up in the middle of the night to see what he was missing online. In fact, he became so engrossed in the virtual world that he shut himself off from peers and parties. The latest gadgets, apps and video games were his true friends.

Ethan's grades began to drop, as he did not turn in all his homework or pay attention in class. He frequently thought about suicide. In his mind, he had become so isolated that no one would even notice he was gone. Suicide would be an escape from all his haunting thoughts. Eventually he even started researching suicide methods online. The thought of taking his life was always in the back of his mind.

When teachers began calling his parents to report his poor performance, they stopped believing his lies about studying and doing homework. They limited his time on the computer, which terrified Ethan. He had nothing to replace that time.

Then one night, two men entered Ethan's room and told him they were taking him to a wilderness camp. His parents had already packed his bags. At this point, Ethan was so depressed he didn't protest and simply went along with the plan.

That camp changed Ethan's life. Cut off from all technology (and most modern comforts), Ethan was forced to converse with other teens, all of whom were suffering from depression and other issues. He had counselors with him who were willing to ask the tough questions, those that made Ethan face his darkest demons. He soon learned that his technology addiction wasn't about technology at all. It was simply a desperate need to escape reality.

After the camp, Ethan began seeing a counselor on a weekly basis, which offered him the opportunity to release the pain he'd been suppressing for so many years. Ethan later graduated with a degree in psychology and currently works at the wilderness camp he attended so many years before.

Fortunately, those close to Ethan were able to recognize signs that he was depressed – even suicidal. Recognizing these signs, whether in yourself or someone you love, is the first critical step in getting better.

Ethan exhibited several of the risk factors and warning signs for suicide and depression. As a victim of bullying, Ethan was more likely to be depressed. In fact, many studies have linked bullying to higher risks of mental health problems during childhood, including low self-esteem, poor school performance, depression and suicide. He isolated himself from his family and friends and turned to technology instead. What Ethan may not have known is that technology addiction is linked to fatigue, stress and even depression and anxiety. Basically Ethan coped with the bullying in ways that were even more detrimental to his health and self-esteem.

Clearly, certain situations can put teens at an increased risk of suicide. Through the stories you've read (and my own, which will follow), I hope you'll recognize that, although not every person with the following risk factors may be depressed or suicidal, that tendency may be greatly exacerbated due to these situations.

Substance Abuse

Your teenage years are a time of discovery. Sometimes, that curiosity includes experimenting with behaviors that may be unhealthy and risky. Chances are, you've already encountered the opportunity to try alcohol or drugs at some point. But did you know that alcohol and drug use makes you more at risk for suicidal thinking and behavior? You already know that depression and mental disorders are the leading cause of suicide in the United States, but guess what? Substance abuse is a close second.

This is because drugs and alcohol interfere with the chemistry of your brain. Misuse of these substances can bring on serious depression. This is especially true for some people who already have a tendency toward depression because of their biology, family history or other life stressors.

Many people who turn to alcohol or drugs are seeking an escape. What they might not know is that the depressive effects of these substances can actually intensify depression. They interfere with the ability to assess risk, make good choices and think of solutions to problems. Many suicide attempts occur when someone is under the influence of alcohol or drugs.

If you're worried that a peer or loved one is abusing drugs or alcohol, you've likely already noticed changes to his or her appearance, personality or behavior. Here are some of the physical and behavioral changes that often come with substance abuse.

Physical warning signs of alcohol and/or drug abuse:

- Bloodshot eyes

- Pupils that are larger or smaller than normal

- Frequent nosebleeds (could be caused by snorted drugs)

- Seizures

- Slurred speech

- Lack of personal hygiene

- Changes in appetite (weight gain or loss)

- Changes in sleep patterns

- Bruises or frequent injuries with no explanation

- Shakes or tremors

Social/behavioral warning signs of alcohol and/or drug abuse:

- Mood swings

- Deterioration of academic performance

- New/different friends or isolation from longtime friends

- Apathy about interests or hobbies that were once important

- Poor concentration, poor memory

- Use of alcohol or drug paraphernalia (bongs, shot glasses, etc.)

- Frequent fights/clashes with family members

- Sudden demand for privacy

- Theft of money, valuables or prescription drugs

- Unusual hyperactivity, anxiety or agitation

As you're about to find out, I have firsthand experience with the dramatic effects of substance abuse. My husband, Bill, used steroids for much of his life. This abuse had a dramatic effect on his mood, temperament and happiness, and significantly contributed to his suicide. How can you tell if someone is using steroids?

Physical warning signs of steroid use:

- testicular atrophy (a medical condition in which testes diminish in size)

- acne

- aggression

- fast muscle growth, rapid weight gain

- greasy hair, oily skin

- small red or purplish acne on the back, shoulders and face

- increased breast tissue (especially in men)

- bad breath

- hair loss

- joint pain

- yellowing of skin

- disrupted sleep

- bloating and night sweats

- nausea and vomiting

- hyperactivity or lethargy

Possible personality changes as a result of steroid use:

- mood swings, irritability

- verbal or physical abuse

- feelings of invincibility

- poor decision-making

- secretiveness, lying

- depression

- withdrawal from family members

- paranoia, hallucinations

Possible social/behavioral changes as a result of steroid use:

- sudden urge to work out at gym

- closed and locked bedroom door

- packages in the mail

- stealing

- napping

- declining grades

- excessive time on internet

My Story

Ok, picture a really perfect-looking football quarterback.

(The kind who would be on the front of a movie poster or something — where even if you don't like watching football or you think you don't like football players, you can't help but stare.)

Then, picture an amazing baseball pitcher.

(Got that image in your mind?)

Next, picture a basketball player sculpted like an action figure.

(Got that one, too?)

This was my husband Bill.

Bill grew up in Houston, Texas and he excelled at all three of these sports. An outstanding athlete, Bill was voted "Best Dressed" and very popular with the girls because he was good looking *and* nice. At six foot two and 150 pounds he was pretty amazing in every way.

Flash forward a couple of years: during Bill's sophomore year of college, his roommate introduces him to bodybuilding. Bodybuilding is a dark sport because it requires an excessive amount of steroid use in order to sculpt your body to look the way a bodybuilder must look. Bill dropped out of college to continue this pursuit, training with Big Phil, who later went on to win the World's Strongest Man competition, weighing in at over 400 pounds.

During this time, Bill added 100 pounds of muscle. You cannot physically put on that kind of size in the gym alone. Steroids became a part of Bill's life – and his personality began to change once he started using them.

"They made me feel like Superman," he said. "I felt like I could do anything I set my mind to."

Yet along with these feelings of superhero-like powers, Bill felt angry. And he took this out on his ex-wife.

He began lying about where he was going and what he was doing.

He stopped calling his parents to check in with them.

He spent at least four hours of every day at the gym, utterly obsessed with his physique.

And in his spare time, he slept.

That sweet, friendly athletic guy everyone loved disappeared. Bill became a monster.

Then in 2001, two brothers, Mike and Ray Mentzer, legends in the bodybuilding world, died two days apart at ages 47 and 49. That might seem old, but it's extremely young. The cause of the deaths was kidney and heart failure caused by years of excessive amounts of steroid use.

"Sad Day for Bodybuilding," read the newspaper headlines.

Today, there are more than 1.5 million teens who admit to using steroids, with the median age for steroid use 15. It is very common in high school athletics; an NCAA survey states that 50 percent of college athletes started steroid use in high school. Girls are actually the largest- growing population with 1 in 20 using.

Even non-athletes use steroids to enhance their personal appearance. These people are called "mirror athletes."

Yet steroid use is very, very dangerous.

For seven years, Bill consumed GHB, a growth hormone steroid, daily. That's well over 2,500 days of his life. It was believed that taking small amounts of this substance helped to increase muscle mass. Apparently everyone in the bodybuilding world used GHB in the hope to get that small edge over their competition. At the time, GHB could be purchased at your local nutrition store.

Today, GHB is referred to as the date rape drug and is an illegal substance.

Eventually, Bill had a job opportunity in California that he wanted to take in order to start a new life. In California, he could no longer purchase GHB, so his body went through the detox process cold turkey. For weeks, Bill suffered nausea, vomiting, cold sweats and insomnia. To battle the insomnia and anxiety, he began taking sleeping pills and sedatives.

In California, Bill's new career as a personal trainer began to take off. Business was thriving, and he acquired enough clientele to open up his own gym. Not long thereafter, a mutual client introduced the two of us.

Love and life are not like a movie, but great first dates and great relationships, particularly in the beginning, can definitely feel like one. There's a reason the expression "feels like you're on cloud nine" exists. When you really hit it off with someone and feel like they get you and you get them *and* you can still be yourself, well, it's an incredible feeling. And that's what it was like when Bill and I met. So two years after we met, we got married. Our wedding day was one of the happiest of my life.

Four years later, the effects of Bill's past began to affect his – and our – present.

First, three people we knew completed suicide.

Big Phil was one of them. His ex-wife called to say he shot himself.

Next was a trainer at the gym, Dave. He rode his motorcycle to a secluded area and shot himself.

And then there was a member of our gym, another guy named Dave. He set himself on fire and jumped off the bluff near our home just two days after he had been in our gym, talking to us about his dreams and struggles.

"What could possibly be so bad in their lives that they would choose to die?" Bill asked. The answer was: probably a lot. Either they were good at hiding it or we didn't know how to read the warning signs.

In 2008, the economy took a big nosedive. Maybe you've heard your parents or other adults talk about it. Or maybe you remember it because it affected you and you remember that mom or dad was out of work or they had to sell your home. Anyway, it was a hard time for us, too. We decided to sell our gym and move to a little condo just south of the California/Mexico border in a town called Rosarito. We had spent many weekends there and took the leap to do a permanent move.

The first three months were awesome – almost like being on a luxurious vacation. We worked out, took Spanish classes, explored the sights, dined out and enjoyed staying in, too. But once summer was over and the tourists went home and the novelty wore off, Bill's insomnia worsened. See, Bill's identity was being a successful gym owner. He needed daily validation that his physique was second to none and a big source of admiration of others, and he was no longer getting that.

He paced our condo, screaming for days, "Get me out of this box! I hate it here!"

This man I loved so deeply had become a virtual stranger to me. He seemed, in fact, unaware of my presence. I knew he was sick and needed help. All of the meds we had did nothing to soothe him. We moved back to California and I searched desperately for a psychiatrist who could help him, but they only changed medications when one wasn't working for his anxiety and sleeplessness. Soon he was taking more than 15 different prescriptions. The layering of all the different medications only made Bill more paranoid and more depressed. Counseling didn't work. Bill was in denial. What he needed was hospitalization and an intensive detox program, but at the time I didn't know it.

Bill said he felt hopeless and worthless. "You would be so much better off without me," he would tell me. "Why do you stay with me?" Bill asked. "All I do is drag you down. I'm just a burden to you."

I called Bill's father to tell him what was happening. He broke down in tears. "Bill has two grandmothers who were hospitalized for depression and—," he said, his voice faltering, "a suicide attempt."

I wouldn't realize the significance of that information until much later. I did know that Bill felt abandoned by his parents, as they had traveled extensively when he was a child and he was often left home alone. He was an only child and was afraid that they would not return. He stayed up and waited, sometimes until the early morning hours. I think that was part of his paranoia with me. He was so afraid that I, too, would leave him.

During this time, Bill struggled just to go to work and train the few clients he had left. He would come home and crawl back into bed. We never did anything social and rarely left the house. I was completely focused on getting him treatment because I so desperately wanted my husband and our lives back. I knew it was just a matter of time before he got better and returned to his old self.

One morning I woke up to find a note Bill had left for me.

Baby,

You need to move on with your life and find somebody better. I can't do this anymore.

Love, Bill

I ran to the bathroom where I could hear him in the shower. "What is this?" I screamed at the top of my lungs.

He confessed he had taken an entire bottle of sedatives as he couldn't handle life anymore. But it didn't work and he had woken up.

Did he really take the entire bottle of pills?

He supposedly consumed more than 20 pills, and yet it did nothing?

I wasn't sure if it was just a cry for attention, but I couldn't risk it. I called my sister and together we persuaded Bill to get in the car with us and drive to Mission Hospital in Laguna Beach. They put him on what is called a "5150" hold, or a three-day involuntary suicide watch. Bill was then released with no treatment.

A few weeks later, Bill left the house early in the morning, didn't say where he was going, and left his phone on the kitchen counter. By early evening, there was still no sign of him. Bill's father called and I told him of my concern and he immediately called and filed a missing persons report. The police came to our apartment, got a description of him, his vehicle and where he may possibly have disappeared to, and started their search. A few minutes later he walked through the front door, completely unaware of the chaos he'd created.

"Where have you been?" I asked, begging my voice to remain steady.

The top of his head was blistered. "Down at the train tracks pacing for the last eight hours," he said. "I needed to get away and have some time to think."

I didn't know it then, but Bill was actually rehearsing his death. He had a plan, but for a different day and time.

Four weeks later, Bill took a turn for the worse. His paranoia skyrocketed – about everything – our finances, where I was every minute of every day, who I was talking to. He rummaged through my closet, looking for signs that I may be seeing someone or having a secret affair.

One night, he trapped me in the bathroom by blockading the door with his outstretched arms.

"What's your secret lover's name?"

"Stop being ridiculous!" I said, "Let me out."

He refused to budge, staring me down.

"Bill, you're scaring me!" I fought my way past him and grabbed my purse. "I love you, but right now I'm afraid of you. I'm going to spend the night at my sister's." I thought spending a night apart would help him realize how ridiculous he was acting and then everything would return to normal.

How wrong I was.

The next morning, I drove home to change clothes and go to work. Bill wasn't at home. I checked my phone and saw multiple missed calls from Bill's parents in Texas.

"I'll tell them not to worry, we're fine, we just needed a little space," I rehearsed in my head. I dialed the number back.

Bill's mother answered.

"Hi, don't worry—-," I began.

"Kristi," she said, her voice flat, detached. "Bill's been in an accident. He's been hit by a train. I think he might be dead."

In shock, I convinced myself that Bill was in his car and the vehicle would have lessened the impact, so hopefully he wasn't badly injured. Bill's father was at a local hotel down the street. Bill had called him the previous morning, told him that he was in trouble and that his brain was scrambled. His dad flew from Houston to San Diego and boarded the train from San Diego to Orange County where we lived.

There was a four-hour delay when the train neared our home. A man had stepped onto the train tracks, spread his arms out to his side like Jesus on the cross and stared into the eyes of the train engineer. At such short notice, the engineer was powerless to stop the train in time and 1,000 tons of steel struck my husband head on. Bill's father, knowing there was an accident but never connecting the dots, sat on the train, wondering what was happening.

It wasn't until the next morning he realized that it had been his son standing in front of that train.

There is Hope

Does that statement sound trite? Maybe. But let's back up. What *is* hope?

Hope is an optimistic attitude based on expectations of positive outcomes in one's life or the world at large.

A person who has a high level of hope has healthier habits, sleeps better, exercises more, eats healthier, gets sick less often and is more likely to have less depression and survive things like cancer.

Students who have hope usually have higher grades. Hope, in fact, is a bigger predictor of who will finish college than SAT or ACT scores.

Hope sounds pretty great, right?

You see, people who are hopeful don't just have a goal, they have a strategy to achieve that goal and the motivation to carry it out. Hope is the belief that the future will be better than the present, and that the power to make it better resides within you.

When you lose hope, it's because you are focusing on obstacles instead of focusing on what excites you. Thinking of something that makes you happy will remind you of what hope feels like. Doing what you do best gives you a boost of confidence and mood. Spending time with hopeful people is also beneficial, because, guess what? Hope is contagious.

The great news is, it's possible to develop hope – even when you think you have none. One way to do this is through a simple exercise. Make a list of people, things and activities that could help you achieve a greater sense of hope. A few examples might be:

- A friend or loved one who believes in you and motivates you

- A favorite activity, sport or hobby you don't want to give up

- A time in your life when you felt whole, happy and loved

- A favorite location, like the beach or your childhood backyard

- An act of kindness someone did for you, or one you performed for someone else

- A favorite song, poem or passage that brings you comfort

- Your belief in a higher power, and what that belief means to you

- Something (or multiple things) you've accomplished through your own efforts

- Something you're looking forward to (an event, vacation, etc.)

Why write these things down? When you have depression, it's easy to forget the things in life that make it worth living, and it's easy to lose your sense of hope. That's because depression is a thief. It *robs* you of hope – hope that you'll feel better, hope that the darkness will lift, hope that the emptiness will fill up and you'll feel motivated and excited again, hope that it won't be like this forever, hope that you'll actually get through it.

Depression has a way of distorting our outlook so that we only notice the bleakest parts of the world. The darkness distorts your reality until it becomes your reality. Depression often robs you of the memory of joy or happiness, so it becomes difficult to draw on happy memories to give you hope for the future.

Many people with depression aren't able to express that they feel hopeless because doing so would require admitting a very real and painful experience. Simply saying, "I feel hopeless" can actually be a positive step. It implies that hope is something that is possible. Negative emotions are suffocating and make it difficult to believe things will get better. You may have lost hope because you feel alone. You may feel like no one understands what you're going through or that you can't talk to anyone.

What do you do when hope feels unfamiliar or impossible? It is important to use a wide variety of coping strategies to help you overcome your depression and look forward to a brand new day – one free of sadness.

First, you need a treatment team and a support system. This includes a therapist, doctor and several friends and family. Ask them to help you remember the times when you felt better and to be in the moment when you do experience joy, even if it's for a few minutes. Participate in activities that you love to do when you're not depressed. Do something that brings you pleasure every day, even if you don't feel like it. Listen to a song you love, watch a favorite old movie or play a sport that makes you feel good. Pleasurable activities actually raise dopamine levels in your brain, causing you to feel better – not to mention these activities will be a welcome distraction from depression, creating glimmers of hope that you *can* feel whole and healthy again. Even though your depression feels like it will last forever, it's important to remind yourself that you are having a depressive episode and it's not a permanent state.

Depression is a liar.

It is an illness that diminishes hope. That is the nature of the disorder. It's important to surround yourself with supportive people so they can help you see through the lies. How hopeless you feel right now does not correlate with how much better you will feel in the future.

Don't overwhelm yourself by expecting too much of yourself too quickly. Make a list of small goals and strive to check something off your list each day. Getting to therapy for help may be one of the items on your checklist. Reach out to supportive loved ones and work hard at not isolating yourself. Take walks, write in a journal. All these things will help to create a more positive outlook.

Create a meditation for hope by listening to soothing background music and writing down, saving and reviewing inspiring quotes. Here are a few to get you started:

What you think or wish, do.

Be your own person because no one can take that away from you.

No one is ever going to be you. Why stop dreaming when you wake up?

Expect only the best from life and take action to get it.

No matter the number of times you fail, keep trying to succeed.

You must not lose hope or faith. Faith and hope work hand in hand.

To be without hope is like being without goals; what are you working toward?

If we expect change, we must act on our hope every day until we have accomplished what we want. With good treatment, effective coping strategies and compassionate support, you will begin to feel better. Your heaviness will get lighter, and your world will become brighter.

So no matter how hopeless you feel right now, please don't give up. Hope and relief are around the corner. They are real, and they are possible.

Commit to yourself and your dreams and take action. If you have doubts about yourself, I hope you'll be able to reevaluate your old beliefs and rediscover the amazing person you are – the one you've always been!

Where to Go

Teenline: 310-855-HOPE or 800-TLC-TEEN

If you have a problem or just want to talk with another teen who understands, this is the right place for you. It's all about teens helping teens. Teenline is a national hotline helping teenagers address their problems before they become a crisis.

This hotline is open from 6 p.m. to 10 p.m. Pacific Time every night. After hours, your call will be directed to Didi Hirsh's Suicide Prevention Center.

TrevorLifeLine (crisis line for LGBTQ youth): 866-488-7386

TrevorText 1-202-304-1200

The Trevor Line is a 24/7 confidential hotline for anyone experiencing suicidal thoughts or crisis. It was specifically developed to help LGBTQ youth.

National Eating Disorders Association: 800-931-2237 *nationaleatingdisorders.org*

This national helpline offers support for youth struggling with any type of eating disorder.

StopBullying.gov

Bullying can be a problem with any age group; parents and schools can help. Learn how to stop bullying by visiting the stop bullying website for resources. *StopBullying.gov*

Substance Abuse Hotline: 800-662-4357 samhsa.gov.

This confidential, 24/7 hotline offers information and treatment options for individuals facing mental and/or substance abuse disorders.

National STD and AIDS Hotline: 800-227-8922 *ashastd.org*

This hotline offers information and resources for anyone facing (or concerned about) AIDS or any other sexually transmitted disease.

National Child Abuse Hotline: 800-4-A-Child (800-422-4453)

Staffed 24/7, this hotline offers crisis intervention and support in over 170 languages for victims of child abuse, or those who suspect the abuse of others.

National Suicide Prevention Lifeline: 800-273-TALK (8255)

Your call will automatically be routed to a trained crisis worker who will listen and can tell you about mental health services in your area. The service is free and confidential, and the line is open 24/7. Everyone should keep this number handy.

The American Foundation for Suicide Prevention: 800-273-8255

This amazing resource is available for anyone with suicidal thoughts or feelings, or those who fear for someone else. It provides information, resources and crisis intervention.

National Alliance of Mental Illness (NAMI) Helpline: 800-950-NAMI (6264)

This hotline provides support, information and referrals to anyone suffering from mental illness.

Crisis Text Line: 741741

When you're not up for talking, help is just a text away at this 24-hour counseling service.

Self-Harm Hotline: 800-273-TALK

This hotline is there to help when you're in crisis, no matter what you're facing.

PTSD Hotline: 800-273-8255

Whether you know you suffer from PTSD or suspect it, this offers a safe space to talk about it.

Thegriefgirl.com

Resources, podcasts and materials on depression, mental illness, grief and suicide from a certified grief counselor and health educator.

Discussion Questions

Listen Up

1. How often do you, your friends or family members talk about suicide, depression or mental illness?

2. What are some things in your life you feel you need to "keep up" with?

3. What would happen if you *didn't* keep up with these things?

4. Have you ever felt like you might have depression?

5. List three things that make you feel *bad* about social media.

6. List three things that make you feel *good* about social media.

7. Which list is easier to make?

What is Depression?

1. What is something new that you learned about depression?

2. Why do you think that most people who complete suicide suffer from depression?

3. Did this chapter make you think of anyone (including yourself) specifically?

4. Why did you think of that person?

5. What are some things you can do to help?

Jackie's Story

1. What are some things Jackie experienced that could cause or worsen depression?

2. Did you relate to anything in Jackie's story?

3. What are some ways Jackie coped with her depression?

4. What could Jackie have done at a younger age to make her life better?

Eating Disorders

1. What's the difference between diet and exercise and an eating disorder?

2. How do you think eating disorders serve as a coping mechanism for other issues?

3. Do you or someone you know have the risk factors or exhibit the symptoms of an eating disorder? What can you do about it?

Ask the Question

1. Have you ever known someone going through a hard time and didn't know what to say (or do)?

2. Can you think of anyone in your life who needs to hear, "R U OK?" right now?

3. If yes, list three people (using initials) you are committed to asking, "R U OK?"

4. What can you do to prepare to listen?

5. Is there an adult you trust if a friend tells you something you need to report?

What's Going on in Your Brain?

1. In what ways do teen brains differ from adult brains?

2. What are some reasons teens tend to be impulsive or reckless?

3. How do you think depression or mental illness can affect your developing brain?

What to Say and What Not to Say

1. If you knew your friend was depressed, what would you do about it?

2. Can you think of a time someone said something to you that made you feel better?

3. Can you think of a time someone said something hurtful that you still remember?

4. What could you say after you've hurt someone's feelings?

What to Do

1. Can you think of any changes you can make that would help you feel better mentally, emotionally and/or physically?

2. Do you get regular exercise and practice good eating habits?

3. Think of someone you can trust to talk to when you're feeling down.

4. How can you relax or unwind when you feel stressed out?

5. Do you know of a friend or family member who could benefit from seeking professional help?

Sofia's Story

In your opinion, why didn't Sofia tell anyone about being bullied?

What are some of the warning signs of suicide Sofia exhibited?

If Sofia was your friend, what would you have done to help?

Bullying

What is the difference between bullying and other altercations/arguments?

Why do you think victims of bullying are more likely to think about suicide?

Have you ever been bullied? Have you ever bullied someone else?

Kaley's Story

1. What social factors do you think influenced Kaley's self-injury?

2. Why do you think Kaley isolated herself from friends and family?

3. How did understanding self-injury empower Kaley to change?

Self-harm

1. How is self-injury different than suicide or suicide attempts?

2. What are some reasons that some people self-injure?

3. What are some of the warning signs or symptoms of self-injury?

4. Why is therapy/counseling so imperative for those who suffer from self-injury?

Post-traumatic Stress Disorder

1. Who suffers from PTSD?

2. How do you know if you have PTSD?

3. What are some of the risks of leaving PTSD untreated?

4. Who would you go to if you thought you had PTSD?

Why Suicide Happens

1. Have you ever heard a friend, family member or peer say anything about having suicidal thoughts?

2. Did you take any action when you heard this?

3. Why do you think some people consider suicide?

4. What would you do if a friend told you they were considering suicide?

Suicide Risk Factors

1. Can you think of anyone in your life that currently displays any of these risk factors?

2. Do you recognize any of the risk factors in yourself?

3. Who can you talk to about a friend or family member that's exhibiting risk factors?

Ethan's Story

1. Have you ever found social media channels or other technologies to be addictive?

2. Do you ever feel isolated or lonely because of this obsession?

3. How can a technology obsession be similar to a drug addiction?

4. Has social media ever made you feel down or depressed? Why?

5. Why do you think the wilderness camp helped treat Ethan's depression?

Substance Abuse

1. What are some of the warning signs of drug and alcohol abuse?

2. Do you know anyone who has taken steroids?

3. Do you think they know the side effects?

4. Were you surprised by any of the steroid side effects mentioned here?

5. Do you ever feel pressured to drink alcohol or take drugs?

6. Why do you think alcohol and drug abuse are linked to depression and suicide?

My Story

1. When do you think Bill first exhibited signs of depression?

2. Do you think Bill made any mistakes after high school? If so, what different choices would you have made?

3. What were some warning signs of steroid use that Bill exhibited?

4. Do you think Bill's steroid use contributed to his depression?

5. What risk factors of suicide did Bill have?

6. What role do you think Bill's prescription drug use played in his suicide?

7. What do you think of Bill's cold-turkey approach for quitting GHB?

8. Do you think having friends complete suicide had an effect on Bill?

9. What suicide warning signs did you find in his behavior?

10. What do you think would have helped Bill?

11. Do you think Bill's upbringing had an impact on him?

12. What advice would you give to a friend thinking about using steroids?

13. If a friend told you that you would be better off without him or her, what would you do?

14. If a friend's behavior scared you, what would you do?

There Is Hope

1. What does hope mean to you?

2. How can you strengthen your sense of hope?

3. Can you think of anyone in your life who needs hope?

4. After reading this book, how can you help?

Acknowledgements

Sheila Peterson   President, Beachside Books, LLC.

Juliet Ekinaka   Cover Design, JDubDesign, Inc.

Kristen Price   Editing

Jane DeLorenzo   Editing

Kelly Brebner   Marketing

Jack Randall   Photography

Ashley Wren-Collins   Editing

For more information about teens in crisis, visit

THEGRIEFGIRL.COM

To reorder **R U OK? Teen Depression & Suicide**, visit

amazon.com

R U OK? Teen Depression & Suicide is brought to you by

Beachside Books

beachsidebooksllc.com